MINIATURE TERRARIUMS

BY FOURWORDS

TUTTLE Publishing

Tokyo | Rutland, Vermont | Singapore

PREFACE

Recreating a plant's natural environment in a transparent glass container, terrariums are a popular way to bring green into homes and work spaces.

Originally devised as a method of transporting plants over an extended period of time, terrariums are now used as a form of small space interior garden, and are often sold at shops selling home goods and furnishings, at specialty garden shops and even at craft stores.

This book shows you how easy it is to make your own small-scale terrariums using moss, ferns, air plants and succulents. Terrariums are fun to look at, fun to create and fun to grow.

And they are very easy to make and care for, once you know how! Play up the characteristics of particular plants and keep the combination of container and plants in mind when creating your very own unique versions.

CONTENTS

WHAT IS A TERRARIUM?

A LITTLE GARDEN, CREATED FOR PLEASURE

THE WARDIAN CASE
The forerunner of the modern terrarium, the Wardian case (c.1829) is a closed protective glass case invented by Nathaniel Bagshaw Ward (1791–1868) in order to shield plants and cocoons from the polluted air of industrial London.

A terrarium is a little garden created for pleasure by cultivating plants in an open or closed transparent container. They're gaining popularity as a source of indoor greenery, as they can be cultivated with minimal watering—light enters the container and, in the case of closed terrariums, moisture evaporates but can't escape, recirculating and thereby recreating the same cycle as in nature.

Terrariums originated in 19th-century London. It was a time when professional plant collectors—known as plant hunters—traveled all over the world in search of rare plants and new species to take back to their own countries. But caring for the collected specimens during transport proved difficult. The "Wardian case," a sometimes elaborate closed glass container, solved the problem. In 1829, physician and passionate horticulture enthusiast Nathaniel Bagshaw Ward sealed a moth's cocoon and some soil in a glass jar and, by coincidence, discovered that a fern and some grass had germinated in the jar. This proved that if soil absorbed water in the contained environment of a glass vessel, it created the conditions necessary for plants' growth, allowing them to be transported for long periods of time.

Since then, various forms of Wardian cases spread among the general populace as they allowed anyone to cultivate and style a small garden with ease. These are now known as terrariums.

Care The more airtight the container, the better the cycle of moisture, meaning that daily watering isn't necessary. Also make sure the terrarium is placed appropriately for the plants inside.

Containers As long as the container is made of transparent glass, which maintains a constant temperature, any shape is fine. There are types with sealable openings and types whose mouths are meant to remain open.

Upgrade your living space Simply adding green to a room makes it a space where you can relax. Why not try incorporating this healing and decorative item into your daily life?

Chapter 1
WETLAND PLANTS

In this book, this category refers to plants that grow at the edge of water or in swampy areas, dislike strong sunlight and require moist soil—including ferns, mosses, butterwort and other carnivorous plants. This category is particularly suited to sealable terrariums.

Mosses

Mosses play a well-known role in bonsai and other types of container gardening. Classified as bryophytes, they grow naturally in various environments such as coastal areas, tropical rainforests, alpine regions and so on. There are over 20,000 species, and most areas where moss grows can boast a number of varieties. Mosses have no roots, with only rhizoids to anchor the leaves, stems and body of the plant. For this reason, most mosses tend to grow densely, spreading out to form a large carpet-like colony to maximize moisture retention and create a support system.

Most mosses are perennials and so can be enjoyed year-round. Their rich green hues exude an air of harmony and healing despite the modest size of the moss.

As moss is unsuited to dry conditions, its leaves wither if it dries out, but it goes into a state of dormancy so there is no cause for concern. It will revive if lightly sprayed with water (a plant mister or spray bottle works well).

Moss requires photosynthesis, so make sure to occasionally place it in soft sunlight to allow it to absorb the sun's rays.

for example

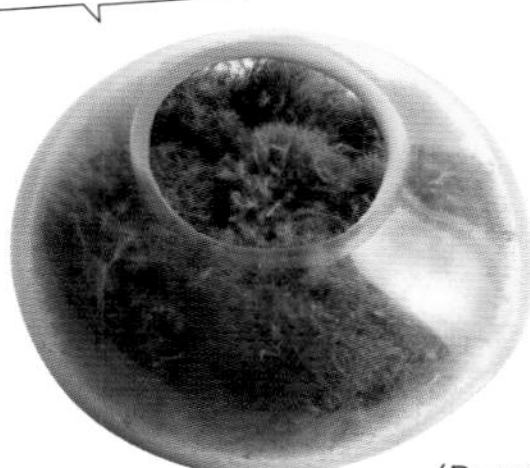

(Page 20)

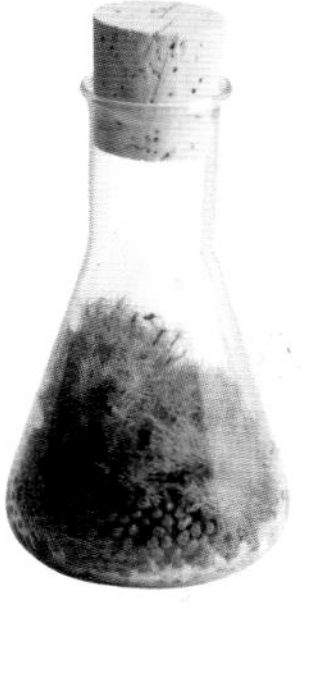

(Page 18)

Chapter 2

TREE-DWELLERS

In this book, "tree-dwelling plants" refers to air plants and epiphytic plants such as orchids which do not put out roots in soil, but rather attach themselves to trees. These plants are characterized by taking in water and nutrients through their leaves and roots in the manner of cutaneous respiration. They are extremely lightweight so are suited to hanging terrariums.

Air Plants

Found widely across the Americas, air plants are members of the genus Tillandsia in the family Bromeliaceae and are related to the pineapple. They get their common name from the fact that they are not rooted in water or soil, but attach themselves to trees, cliffs and so on.

As they require no soil, they lend themselves to all kinds of arrangements. They can be affixed to driftwood or to a brick wall, or planted in any sort of container. Their roots serve mainly to anchor them in place, while trichomes—hair-like structures on the surface of the leaves—absorb moisture and nutrients.

Air plants can loosely be subdivided into silver-leaved types, so called because the leaves are covered with so many trichomes that they appear white, and green-leaved types which have few trichomes or none at all.

As air plants naturally grow in regions where wet and dry seasons are clearly defined, they can tolerate extremes. However, they are actually lovers of moisture, so it is important to water them regularly. Additionally, they like windy conditions and so prefer to be outdoors. Finding a spot out of direct sunlight where they will receive dappled light is ideal.

for example

(Page 40)

(Page 34)

Chapter 3
ARID ZONE PLANTS

In this book, this category encompasses succulents such as those in the Haworthia and Echeveria genera along with cacti that have evolved to have the capacity to store water and thrive in harsh, dry environments. They are suited to partially sealed or permanently open terrariums.

Succulents

Distributed densely across southern Africa, succulents grow naturally in areas such as those with wet and dry seasons that approximate desert conditions and on cliff faces in mountainous regions. As there is little rainfall where they grow, these fleshy plants store moisture in their leaves, stems and roots.

Around 50 families of plants are included in this category. Their individualistic appearances and textures make them popular with collectors. Many types have leaves that change color to a beautiful red between fall and winter, so they offer broad scope for group planting.

However, because growth patterns differ, it's important to choose the right environment for each plant. Summer growers grow from spring through to fall; winter growers from fall through to spring; and spring/fall growers grow in spring and fall.

Adding to succulents' appeal is the fact that they can be multiplied easily, either by taking a cutting from a larger plant and cultivating it in a separate pot, or by planting a leaf removed from the main plant.

for example

(Page 76)

(Page 54)

TOOLS

Here, we present the tools used when creating terrariums. You can use items to hand in place of some of these, so use your ingenuity when it comes to choosing your tools.

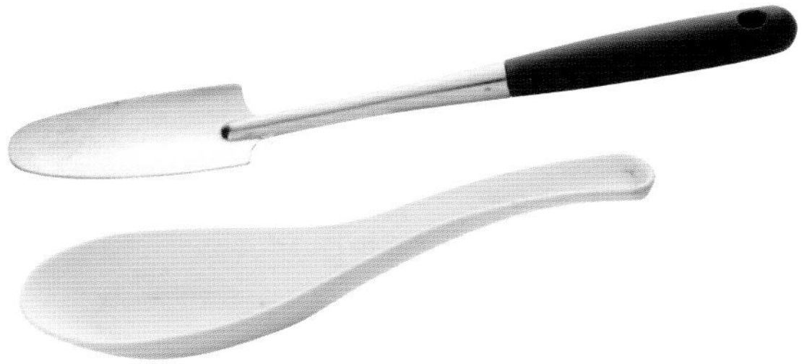

Trowel
This is used to secure plants into soil. A metal spoon or Chinese-style soup spoon works as a substitute.

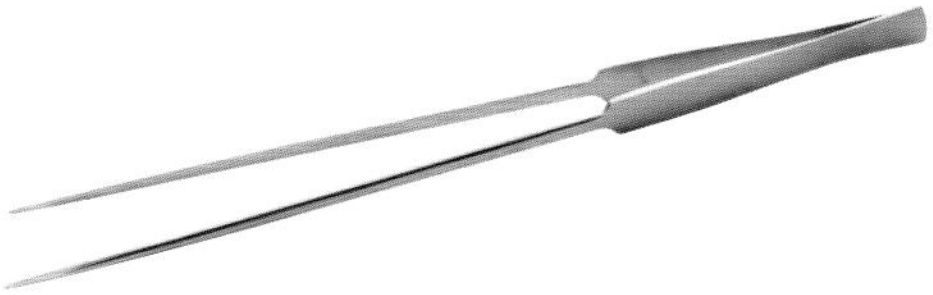

Tweezers
Used for planting small plants or adjusting plants' position. Long tweezers are handy for planting in a terrarium with a narrow opening.

Funnel
Used for pouring soil into the terrarium. You can make a substitute by rolling a durable sheet of paper or plastic into a narrow-ended tube.

Watering Can
Water along the edge of the glass container so that the composition inside the terrarium is not disturbed. A long, narrow spout is recommended.

Spray Bottle
This is used when plants need to be completely covered in water. It is also useful when applying a light liquid fertilizer or for winter watering when only a light spray is needed.

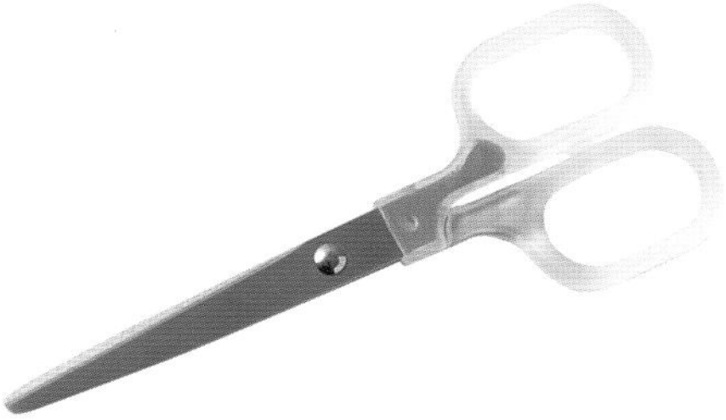

Scissors
Used for trimming roots and leaves from potted plants to prepare them for planting in a terrarium. Specialist gardening scissors are not necessary—regular scissors are fine.

MAKING A TERRARIUM

BASIC INSTRUCTIONS (USING SUCCULENTS)

Terrariums are simple to make, even for beginners. To start off, let's try making one using succulents. Once you've got the hang of things, you can try choosing different containers, plants, soils and so on.

Plants to use

Sedum rubrotinctum
Sedum pachyphyllum
Echeveria simonoasita

You will need

Container
Seramis granules
Pumice (medium size granules
Natural stones (medium size, white)

Wash container
Bacteria can have a negative effect on plants' health, so wash the container carefully and dry it thoroughly before use.

Add pumice
Place pumice (see page 13) at the base of the container. A funnel or Chinese soup spoon is helpful for directing the pumice. Here the pumice is about 3/8 inch (1cm) deep.

Add Seramis
Pour Seramis (see page 13) on top of the pumice. In this example, Seramis has been used for its sterile, odorless qualities, but regular gardening soil is fine too.

Prepare plants
Brush a little soil from the roots and trim excess roots using scissors. If using a cutting, place it in shade a few days beforehand to dry it out.

Decide on positioning of plants
Decide where to position plants in the terrarium. Planting and then removing plants can damage them, so have an image of the finished result in mind before planting.

Begin with large plants
Once their position has been decided, start by planting larger plants. Use a trowel or funnel to aim Seramis around the roots to secure plants in place.

Use tweezers for small plants
Tweezers and the like come in handy when planting smaller plants. Use them when planting cuttings too, making sure not to grip plants too firmly.

Add natural stones
Add a layer of natural stones (see page 13 for these and other gravels and soils). Try using different colored stones, crushed coral, bark chips and so on to create different surface textures.

Adjust overall balance
To finish, use tweezers to neaten the layers, remove debris such as dead leaves and adjust plants' positions. Watering will help settle the plants..

TIPS

Types of soil
(see page 13)

- For moss, use charcoal or porous ceramic medium which retains water well.
- For succulents, Kanuma pumice, akadama soil, vermiculite and other horticultural soils that drain well are suitable.
- Air plants may simply be placed on top of pumice, crushed coral and so on. They also thrive if bound to driftwood, cork, palm fiber and the like.

WATERING

All plants—even those from arid regions—require a certain amount of water. The frequency of watering, the amount of water needed each time and other factors vary greatly depending on plant type and conditions.

Moss (Wetlands)

Mosses like soil that is constantly moist, so it's fine if a few millimeters of water collect at the base of the container. Use a spray bottle to make sure the whole plant is covered. Mosses like humidity, but too much watering can cause mold to develop. If there seems to be too much moisture in the container, remove the lid to let excess moisture evaporate, and adjust watering patterns to ensure healthy humidity levels.

Air Plants (Tree Dwellers)

It is often mistakenly thought that air plants can do without watering, but they actually love water. For this reason, apart from wintertime, daily watering is ideal. Mist the air plants to the point that they drip. If the leaf ends wither or seem wrinkly, or you notice other signs that indicate inadequate levels of water, submerge the entire plant in a container of water for around six hours (this is known as soaking).

Succulents (Arid Regions)

As they are plants which originate from arid regions, succulents store large amounts of water in their leaves, so can generally thrive without daily watering. Depending on the season and type, some may not require watering for an entire month, and some may even be damaged from over watering. It's important to be aware of the succulent's type and to water according to the plant's particular characteristics.

SOILS • ORNAMENTAL GRAVEL

Here you'll find the types of soil suited to terrariums. Of course regular horticultural soil is fine too.

Main types of planting medium and ornamental gravel

❶ Natural stones (white, medium)
In this book, stones of about $\frac{7}{8}$–$1\frac{1}{8}$ inch (2–3cm) are used. White natural stones are the perfect complement to vivid green plants.

❷ Natural stones (white, small)
These are about $\frac{1}{8}$–$\frac{1}{4}$ inch (3–5mm) in size. Their small size makes them suited to layering to achieve overall balance.

❸ Crushed coral (small)
Each piece of this coral is about $\frac{1}{4}$–$\frac{3}{8}$ inch (5–10 mm). It is suited to recreating the arid region scenery appropriate for succulents, air plants and the like.

❹ Natural stones (gray, medium)
In this book, stones of about $\frac{7}{8}$–$1\frac{1}{8}$ inch (2–3cm) are used. These work well in both arid region type terrariums and wetland terrariums.

❺ Natural stones (gray, small)
In this book, stones of about $\frac{1}{8}$–$\frac{1}{4}$ inch (3–5mm) are used. They work well with moss, succulents, air plants and any other type of plant.

❻ Crushed coral (medium)
Larger pieces of coral are crushed to create this type of gravel. The texture lends it to surface decoration, providing an accent in the terrarium.

❼ Bark
Tree bark is finely crushed to create this material. Simply strewing this over the surface as a finishing touch makes a big difference in the look of a terrarium.

❽ Natural stones (purple)
The purple of these natural stones is a good match for the pale shades of succulents such as Sedams and Echeverias.

❾ Fuji sand
This is volcanic ash that has been processed into a medium for gardening. It holds water well, so is suitable for terrariums with moss and other wetland plants.

White silicate
This planting medium is packed with minerals and helps to purify water and soil. It is also effective in preventing root decay.

Granulated planting medium
This medium is made from charcoal coated with porous ceramic. It retains water well, and in this book is used for wetland plants.

Seramis
This planting medium contains nutrients and is sterile and odorless. It breathes and drains well, making it well suited to terrariums.

Pumice
This pumice for horticultural use breathes and drains well, so is recommended as the bottom layer for a terrarium. It comes in various sizes.

SEASONAL CARE

Every plant has environments in which it does well—and environments in which it does not. If plants are cultivated in environments that replicate their natural habitats they will grow and grow. When they outgrow their container, enjoy transplanting them into a larger container or trimming them to grow more plants from the cuttings.

Wetland Plants

These environments prefer year-round moisture, so the key to maintaining these terrariums is careful daily watering, apart from in mid-winter. If placed in direct sunlight the temperature inside the container will become too high and damage the plants, so keep them out of strong sun in summer and make sure that even during the rest of the year they are placed only in areas of light shadow.

Air Plants

Spring through to fall is the growth period for air plants, so it's best to place them in an environment of dappled light and give them plenty of water. Regardless of the season, keep them out of direct light. Particularly during harsh summer periods, place them in shade where air can circulate well. Gentle sunlight filtered through a curtain is ideal. Watch out for dehydration during winter. Place them outside about once a week where they can catch the breeze, and make sure to water them.

Succulents

These plants grow naturally in arid regions with harsh sunlight. For this reason, if they do not receive enough sun, their stems can wither and leaves may be damaged, so be sure to place them where the sun can reach them. In summer, humidity increases, so cut down on direct sunlight and watering and place them in a well-ventilated area. These plants do not cope well with cold, so in winter make sure they are placed in a warm spot.

Chapter 1

WETLAND PLANTS

Moss is the main feature of these terrariums whose compositions conjure verdant wetland areas. A flask, test tube or other lidded container that's slightly different from the norm is ideal for housing moss, which requires soil that is constantly moist.

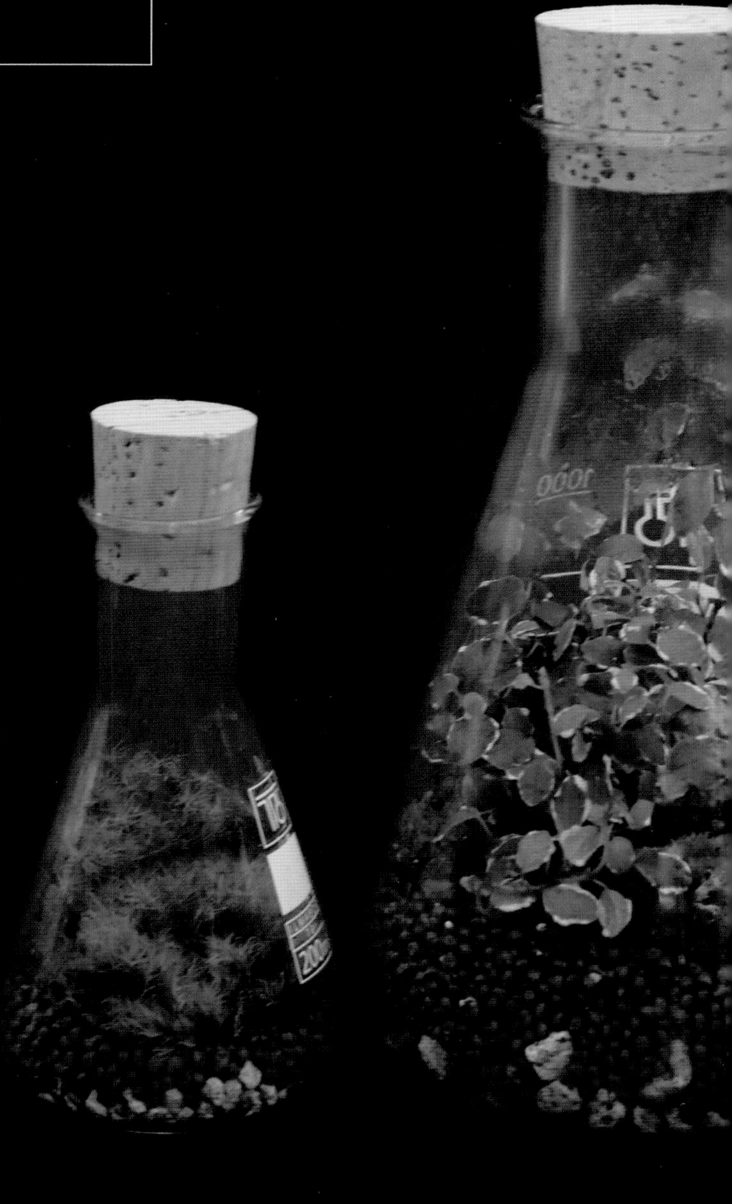

A TERRARIUM WITH FLUFFY SELAGINELLA

Also known as cushion moss, this plant is not actually a moss, but a member of the fern family. Its appeal lies in its soft, fluffy texture which looks so temptingly tactile and is well-suited to a container with roundness of form.

Layout

Instructions

1 Pour a small amount of silicate into the container, then cover with a layer of pumice to form a base.

2 Decide on the height of the plants within the container, then add granular medium around plants with potting medium still attached.

3 Position plants in center of container and add planting medium to secure plants. a

Plants to use

Selaginella—a

You will need

Jar-type glass container
White silicate soil (such as pumice)
Pumice (medium grain)—b
Granular medium based on charcoal and porous ceramic material—c

TIPS

- Keep out of direct sunlight and place in a bright but shaded area or a room which gets plenty of natural light.
- Although they are susceptible to becoming dried out, mosses do not like too much humidity either, so be sure to give them adequate air.

ILMABOR
TGI
200ml

Plant Type

Moss

A CONICAL FLASK TERRARIUM OF LUSH MOSSES

The conical flasks used in chemistry experiments are ideally suited as terrarium containers. It's easy to monitor the conditions inside and if stoppered, the temperature can be kept constant.

Layout

Plants to use

[A]
Bryum argenteum—a
Ficus pumila—b

[B]
Polytrichum juniperinum—c

[C]
Selaginella—e
Rainbow fan (selaginella uncinata)—d

You will need

Conical flasks
White silicate soil
Pumice (small grains)—f
Granular medium made from charcoal and porous ceramic material—g

Instructions

1 Place a small amount of white silicate soil into each container, then cover with a layer of pumice to form a base.

2 Add granular medium around plants with potting medium still attached to form two layers.

3 Secure all plants except for moss, then use tweezers to add moss. a

4 Finish by using tweezers to adjust the overall composition. b

TIPS

- Flasks have narrow openings, so work slowly and carefully when adding or removing the plants to avoid damage.
- Keep out of direct sunlight and place near a window where the light is about as bright as that filtered through lace curtains.

Plant Type

Moss

NATURAL DRIFTWOOD PAIRED WITH A TERRARIUM MAKES A UNIQUE DISPLAY ITEM

In this terrarium the shape of the glass creates an impression. Both the container and the driftwood have their own particular presence, so it's best to go for a simple plant arrangement inside. An elliptical container like this one looks most attractive when the center is built up high to create volume.

Layout

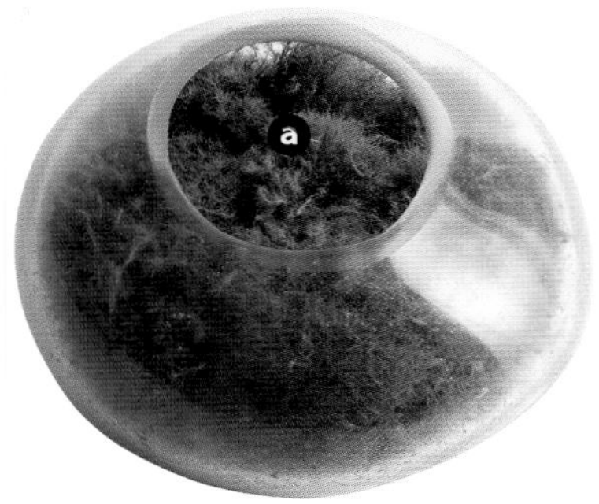

Plants to use

Bartramia pomiformis—a

You will need

Piece of driftwood and round glass container, preferably somewhat irregular
Granular medium
White silicate (such as pumice)

Instructions

1 Pour a small amount of silicate into the container, then adjust height using granular medium.

2 Work from the sides of the container towards the center to spread moss over the soil surface. a

3 Complete by planting moss at the center. b

4 Spray with water to allow moss to settle in.

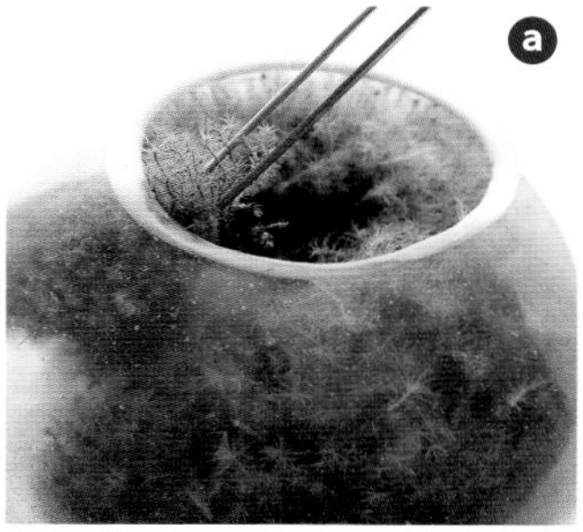

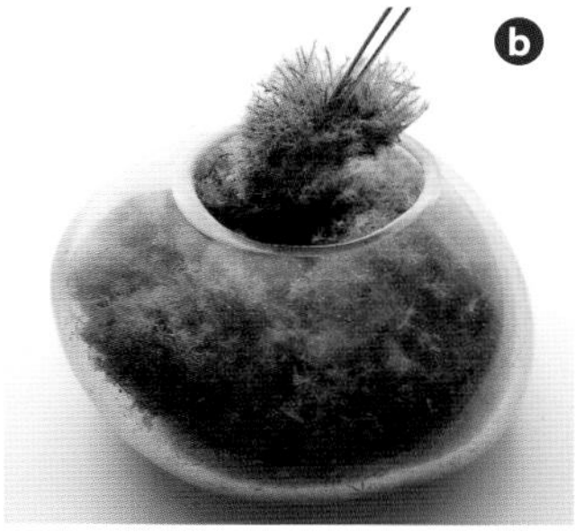

TIPS

- Adjust the amount of soil clinging to the rhizoids of the moss so that the moss is raised in the center.
- Although they are susceptible to becoming dried out, mosses do not like too much humidity either, so be sure to give them adequate air.

TEST TUBE TERRARIUMS MAKE MONITORING THE PLANTS' DAILY DEVELOPMENT FUN

Although they appear similar at first glance, each type of moss has its own characteristics. Line up different kinds and enjoy watching how they grow. Test tubes are also good for little succulents or aquatic plants.

Layout

Plants to use

Selaginella—a
Hypnaceae—b
Bartramia pomiformis—c

You will need

Test tubes
Test tube stand
White silicate soil (such as pumice)
Granular medium made from charcoal and porous ceramic material—d

Instructions

1 Pour a small amount of silicate into each test tube.

2 Roughly decide the height at which you want plants to sit and pour in granular medium around plants, which still have potting mix attached.

3 Complete by using tweezers to position plants in the test tube. a

TIP

- Keep out of direct sunlight and place near a window where the light is about as bright as that filtered through lace curtains.

Plant Type

Ferns

A PAIRING OF FERN AND ASPARAGUS FOR A REFRESHING FEEL

Here, a pairing of Selaginella with highly compatible Asparagus fern which, despite its common name, is actually a vine plant. The fluffy Selaginella and delicate Asparagus fronds give a feeling of airy freshness.

Layout

Plants to use

Selaginella—a
Asparagus fern—b

You will need

Jar-type glass container
White silicate soil (such as pumice)
Pumice—c
Granular medium made from charcoal and porous ceramic material—d

Instructions

1 Place a small amount of white silicate soil into the container, then cover with a layer of pumice to form a base.

2 Decide on the height of each plant within the container, then add granular medium around plants with potting medium still attached.

3 Secure the tall Asparagus at the back of the arrangement with the Selaginella at the front.

4 Finish by using tweezers to adjust the overall composition. a

TIPS

- Keep out of direct sunlight and place in a bright but shaded area or in a room that gets plenty of bright natural light.
- Apart from during midsummer, asparagus enjoys occasionally receiving sunlight.

CARNIVOROUS PLANTS JOIN SWAMP-LOVERS IN A TERRARIUM GROUP PLANTING

Popular carnivorous plants star in this recreation of a swampland scene. Humidity-loving plants are well suited to terrariums. Create visual interest and a natural atmosphere by using plants of different heights.

Layout

Plants to use

Pteris—a
Butterwort—b
Hypnaceae—c

You will need

Jar-type glass container
White silicate soil
Pumice (medium grain)—d
Granular medium made from charcoal and porous ceramic material—e

Instructions

1 Place a small amount of white silicate soil into the container, then cover with a layer of pumice to form a base.

2 Decide on the height of the plants within the container, then add granular medium around plants with potting medium still attached.

3 Decide where the front will be, then, working from the back of the container, securely plant Pteris and then butterwort.

4 Use tweezers to add moss.

5 Finish by using tweezers to adjust the overall composition.

TIPS

- Keep out of direct sunlight and place near a window where the light is about as bright as that filtered through lace curtains.
- Make sure the terrarium does not dry out (see page 12).

Plant Type

Saintpaulia

ENJOY BEAUTIFUL BLOOMS YEAR-ROUND WITH AN AFRICAN VIOLET TERRARIUM

The humidity-loving African violet is well suited to terrariums and is an appealing choice, as its flowers can be enjoyed nearly all year round. If it's in a spot that doesn't get much light, it can be grown using only a grow-light.

Layout

Plants to use

African violet—a

You will need

Multifaceted glass terrarium
White silicate soil
Granular medium
Perlite —b

Instructions

1 Place a small amount of white silicate soil into the container, then add perlite.

2 Position plant in center of container, then add granular medium around plant with potting medium still attached. Add perlite around plant to secure it and complete the terrarium. a

TIPS

- Keep out of direct sunlight and place in a bright spot near a window.
- These plants do not like cold or heat, so temperature monitoring is vital.
- African violets are susceptible to gray mold (Botrytis cinerea) so apply a fungicide or similar treatment to the leaves before planting.

practical tip

1

WHERE TO OBTAIN MOSS

Whether planted alone or as part of a group, moss adds vivid color to a terrarium. Here are some places where it can be obtained.

BUY IT AT A GARDENING STORE

Moss is available at gardening stores, and it is convenient to buy it there if you need large amounts at a time or are looking for a particular type. Depending on what the store carries, you may be able to find some unusual varieties. Being able to choose textures and shades of moss to suit your own taste is another advantage of shopping at a gardening store. When selecting, be sure to consider how the moss will work with the other plants in the terrarium.

COLLECT IT FROM A PARK

Moss grows in many places familiar to us, such as by the side of footpaths and cracks in concrete walls and sidewalks. In parks, fine specimens can be obtained from under trees or on the ground where foot traffic is minimal. For neat results, use a tool like a spatula to scoop it up or prise it off the ground with a trowel. Concrete-loving types such as Bryum argenteum and Hypnaceae can be obtained from gaps in asphalt.

COLLECT IT FROM A FOREST

It takes time and effort, but moss gathered from a forest cannot be beaten for its color and form. Some forest areas are private property or they may be a conservation area where gathering plants is prohibited, so when planning to obtain moss from a forest, do your homework and exercise care and consideration. Taking too much can damage the natural regeneration cycle so it's important to keep to small amounts to avoid disrupting the ecosystem.

Chapter 2

AIR PLANTS

Dwelling largely in trees, air plants can be quite at home in the right terrarium. Air plants like breezy conditions, so they suit hanging containers, which allow both good ventilation and a variety of styling possibilities.

Plant Type

Tillandsia

Layout

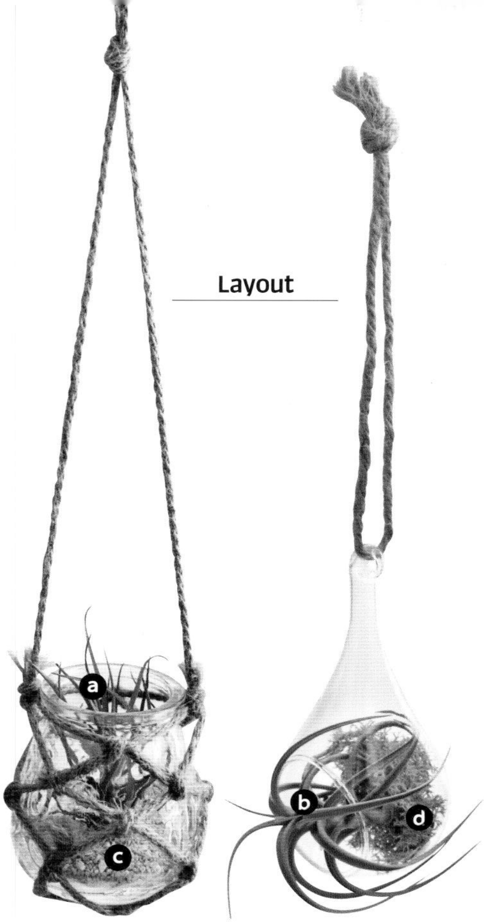

SIMPLE HANGING TERRARIUMS YOU CAN MAKE RIGHT NOW

Simply put an air plant in a glass bottle or empty glass jar and hang it as a decoration to transform any room. It's an easy way to add green in areas with little space, such as a small kitchen or bathroom.

Instructions

1 Pour coral (or dried moss) into container.

2 Add air plant. (a)(b)

3 Finish by using tweezers or other tools to adjust the overall composition.

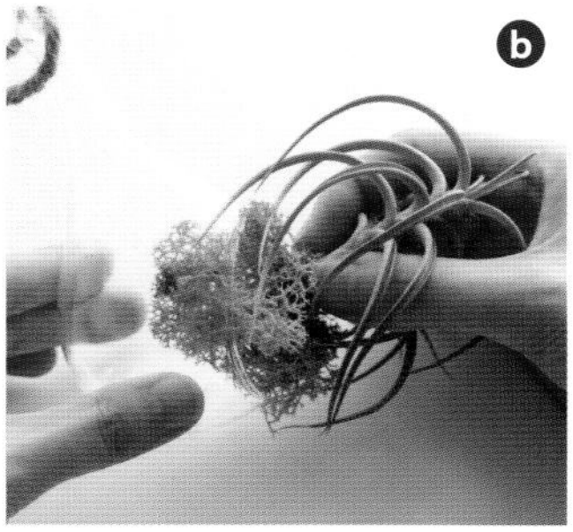

Plants to use

Tillandsia ionantha—(a)
Tillandsia aeranthos—(b)

You will need

Hanging glass container
Linen cord
Crushed coral (small)—(c)
Moss (dried moss)—(d)

TIPS

- Try different glass containers and cords to create different effects.
- Keep out of direct sunlight, ideally near a window where air flows well and the light is about as bright as that filtered through lace curtains.
- During their growth period, take them outdoors and soak them (page 12).

Plant Type
Tillandsia

ADD NATURAL ELEMENTS FOR A TROPICAL RESORT-STYLE TERRARIUM

It's difficult to get a sense of a particular season from air plants, so make use of natural materials to expand their repertoire. If it's a summer look you're after, driftwood, shells and so on are useful additions to create atmosphere.

Layout

Plants to use

Tillandsia pohliana—ⓐ
Tillandsia ionantha—ⓑ

You will need

Spherical class container
Walnut shell chips—ⓒ
Coconut husk—ⓓ

Instructions

1 Place walnut shell chips in container.

2 Place coconut husk in container and add air plants in, working from back to front. ⓐⓑ

3 Finish by using tweezers or other tools to adjust the overall composition.

TIPS

- Keep out of direct sunlight and place in soft light about the same brightness as sunlight dappled through leaves. If keeping indoors, place near a window where air flows well and the light is about as bright as that filtered through lace curtains.
- During the growth period from spring through to fall, remove from container. Placed outdoors in a well ventilated area and watered thoroughly, they will thrive.

Plant Type

Tillandsia

A CHIC RED TILLANDSIA CAPITATA FOR AN ELEGANT VASE TERRARIUM

Chic red leaves point straight up from the Tillandsia capitata. Allowing the leaves to extend out beyond the mouth of the vase lends a different sort of spatial effect. Pairing it with Tillandsia usneoides (Spanish moss) adds a little graceful refinement.

Layout

Instructions

1 Place coral, chips and then coral in the container to form layers. a

2 Place first usneoides and then capitata in the container and adjust for a neat finish. b

Plants to use

Tillandsia capitata—a
Tillandsia usneoides (Spanish moss)—b

You will need

Glass vase
Crushed coral (medium)—c
Walnut shell chips—d

TIPS

- These varieties are particularly vulnerable to dehydration so care is needed in the dry winter months.
- Keep out of direct sunlight and place in soft light about the same brightness as sunlight dappled through leaves. If keeping indoors, place near a window where air flows well and the light is about as bright as that filtered through lace curtains.
- From spring through to fall, remove from container and water thoroughly.

Plant Type

Tillandsia

A DIAMOND-SHAPED HANGING TERRARIUM DOUBLES AS A DELICATE TREE ORNAMENT

The simpler the terrarium, the more important it is to choose an air plant that complements the container. How about a Tillandsia bulbosa, with its green leaves that resemble untamable hair? Its shape is perfect for a tall, narrow hanging terrarium like this one.

Layout

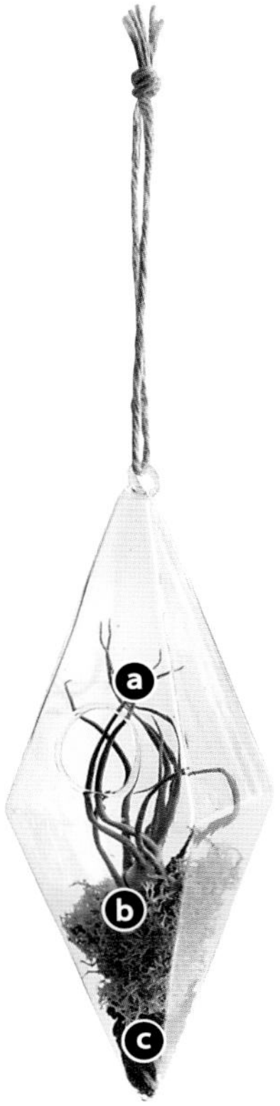

Plants to use

Tillandsia bulbosa—a

You will need

Vertical hanging glass container
Linen cord
Moss (dried moss)—b
Walnut shell chips—c

Instructions

1 Place walnut shell chips and dried moss in container.

2 Use tweezers to add air plant and adjust overall composition to complete the terrarium.

TIPS

- Try different glass containers and cords to create different effects.
- This variety is particularly vulnerable to dehydration so care is needed in the dry winter months.
- Keep out of direct sunlight and place near a window where air flows well and the light is about as bright as that filtered through lace curtains.

CLIFF

Plant Type

Tillandsia

A SELF-CONTAINED DESERT OASIS

When skillfully cultivated and tended, air plants can flower. The little flowers inside the vivid pink "quills" last only a few days, but the quills themselves can be enjoyed for several weeks or months. To incorporate scenery into the composition, a spherical container works best.

Layout

Plants to use

Tillandsia tenuifolia—a
Tillandsia ionantha—b
Tillandsia fuchsii var gracilis—c

You will need

Spherical glass container
Crushed coral (medium)—d
Moss (dried moss)—e

Instructions

1 Add crushed coral and dried moss, creating different heights.

2 Add taller air plants at the back of the container.

3 Use tweezers to adjust composition and complete the terrarium.

TIPS

- Keep out of direct sunlight and place in soft light about the same brightness as sunlight dappled through leaves. If keeping indoors, place near a window where air flows well and the light is about as bright as that filtered through lace curtains.
- Occasionally remove from container and give plant plenty of water (see page 12).

Plant Type

Tillandsia

SIMPLE TERRARIUMS DISPLAYED TOGETHER AS INTERIOR ACCENTS

Simple cylindrical glass containers are popular as they are easy to handle even for beginners. Keep things simple in smaller ones by placing just one type of plant in each and enjoy grouping the containers together. Go for a selection of different finishes.

Layouts

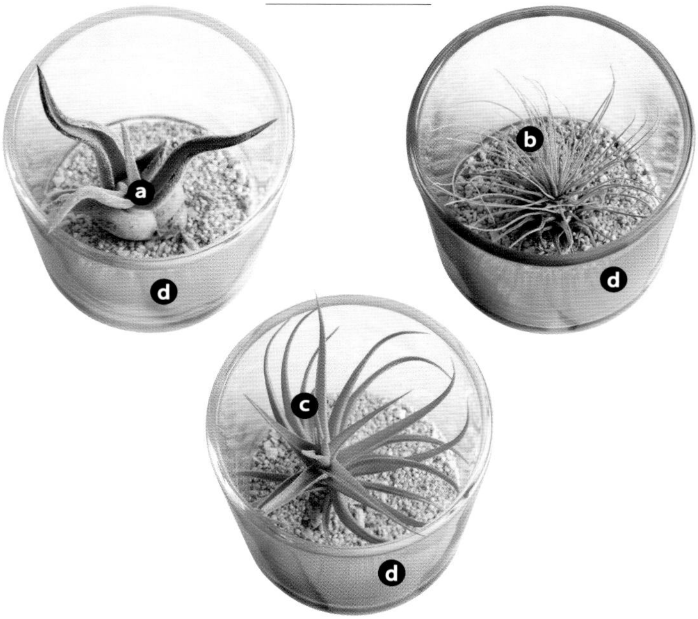

Plants to use

Tillandsia caput-medusae—a
Tillandsia fuchsii var gracilis—b
Tillandsia aeranthos—c

You will need

Cylindrical glass container
Crushed coral (small)—d

Instructions

1 Decide how high in the container the air plant will sit and pour crushed coral in.

2 Use tweezers to place air plant in container and neaten composition to complete the terrarium. a b

TIPS

- Keep out of direct sunlight and place in soft light about the same brightness as sunlight dappled through leaves. If keeping indoors, place near a window where air flows well and the light is about as bright as that filtered through lace curtains.

Plant Type

Tillandsia

USING UNUSUAL SHAPES TO CREATE CHIC LOOKS: A LIGHT BULB TERRARIUM

Terrariums allow you to experiment with unusual items at hand. With great care and attention to safety, incandescent light bulbs can be opened and emptied. Alternatively, light bulb-shaped containers made of thicker, safer glass are available for purchase, and are perfect for housing an original miniature garden.

Layout

Plants to use

Tillandsia andreana—a
Tillandsia aeranthos—b
Tillandsia cyanea—c

You will need

Light bulb-shaped container and a round-interior base
Crushed coral (medium)—d

Instructions

1 Place container on a base/stand as you work.

2 Pour in crushed coral in a shade that sets off the plant.

3 Use tweezers to add air plants, working from the back, then adjust overall composition. a

TIPS

- If the coral slides out of place, shake the container gently to restore balance and adjust the container's position in the base accordingly.
- Leave open during the day to allow air in and cover opening at night so that moisture recirculates.
- Keep out of direct sunlight and place near a window where air flows well and the light is about as bright as that filtered through lace curtains.

A CHARMING ANTIQUE LANTERN WITH A GROUP OF THREE SILVER-LEAVED PLANTS

Air plants work well with uniquely-shaped glass cases. In particular, the cool silver-leaved types compliment an antique container. The trick is to trail the Spanish moss out of the container to add dimension.

Layout

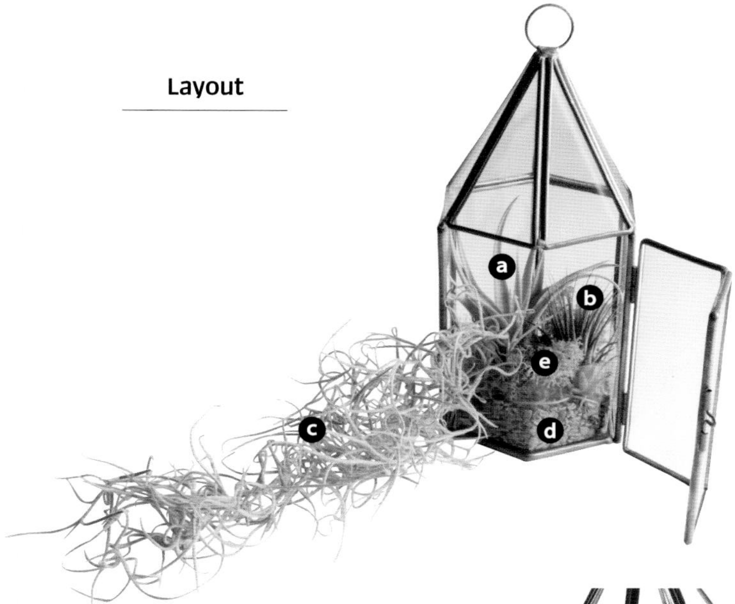

Plants to use

Tillandsia harrisii—a
Tillandsia ionantha—b
Tillandsia usneoides (Spanish moss)—c

You will need

Glass gazebo terrarium
Walnut shell chips—d
Moss (dried moss)—e

Instructions

1 Place walnut shell chips in container.

2 Working from the back, place dried moss, harrisii, ionantha and more dried moss in the container in that order. a b

3 Use tweezers to adjust composition.

4 Place Spanish moss in the front of the container and trail it out to complete the terrarium.

TIPS

- Leave open during the day to allow air in and close as much as possible at night so that moisture recirculates.
- Keep out of direct sunlight and place in soft light about the same brightness as sunlight dappled through leaves. If keeping indoors, place near window where air flows well and the light is about as bright as that filtered through lace curtains.
- Spanish moss is particularly vulnerable to dehydration so care is needed in the dry winter months.

Plant Type

Tillandsia

Layout

A SPHERICAL HANGING TERRARIUM

A lush little terrarium hangs from a curtain rod, swaying in the breeze coming through an open window. This creates a cool effect, perfect for summer.

Plants to use

Tillandsia stricta—ⓐ

You will need

Hanging glass container
Linen cord
Walnut chips—ⓑ
Moss (dried moss)—ⓒ

Instructions

1 Decide on the layout, then place walnut chips and dried moss in the container. ⓐ

2 Use tweezers to add air plant and adjust the composition to complete the terrarium. ⓑ

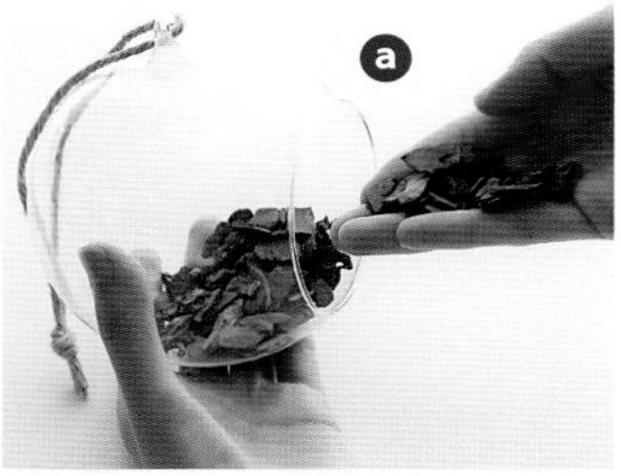

TIPS

- Try different glass containers and cords to create different effects.
- Keep out of direct sunlight and place near a window where the light is about as bright as that filtered through lace curtains.

A TERRARIUM ON A STAND AS OBJET D'ART

A terrarium on a stand is packed with interior design potential. It presents a stylish image, and the vibrant frond-like flowers of this plant add a whole new array of charms. The effortless draping of Spanish moss perfects the picture.

Layout

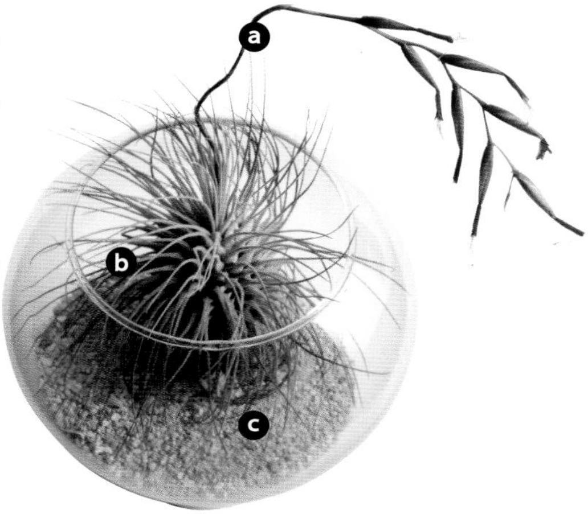

Plants to use

Tillandsia fuchsii var gracilis—ⓐ
Tillandsia usneoides (Spanish moss)—ⓑ

You will need

Container and compatible stand. Be sure that the stand is stable and able to firmly hold the container.
Crushed coral (small)—ⓒ

Instructions

1 Decide how high the plant will sit and pour crushed coral into the container.

2 Use tweezers to add Tillandsia fuchsii var gracilis and adjust the composition. ⓐ

3 Place finished terrarium on stand.

4 Trail Spanish moss over stand.

TIPS

- Keep out of direct sunlight and place in soft light about the same brightness as sunlight dappled through leaves. If keeping indoors, place near a window where the air flows well and the light is about as bright as that filtered through lace curtains.
- Spanish moss is particularly vulnerable to dehydration so care is needed in the dry winter months.

practical tip
2

WHERE TO DISPLAY YOUR TERRARIUMS

It's important to choose a spot for your terrariums where the plants will thrive. The trick is to display them attractively in the environment most suited to them.

PLACE THEM BY A WINDOW TO CREATE A GREEN INTERIOR VIBE

Placed by a window where it receives curtain-filtered sunlight, a terrarium is an eye-catcher that adds both calm and energy to a room. Most of the plants in this book do not like direct sunlight, so try growing them by a window where the light is softer. The color of succulents such as Haworthia is enhanced when they receive sunlight. It's also important that plants be placed in a well ventilated spot. Monitor plants to be sure the environment is as friendly to their growth as it is pleasing to the eye.

HANGING TERRARIUMS IS A GREAT WAY TO SAVE SPACE

Cord such as linen that can be braided using macramé techniques allows terrariums to be hung for display. Air plants and other plants that don't require soil are light and require little maintenance, making them ideal for displaying in hanging containers. These terrariums can dangle from a stand or a curtain rod, or from hooks attached to rafter or ceiling. A group of hanging terrariums can make a very attractive display.

Chapter 3

ARID ZONE PLANTS

These terrariums feature succulents—supple plants that store water and love sunlight. The use of gravel, driftwood and other elements that evoke an arid region lends a natural look and feel. Enjoy combining these super-sweet succulents with various planting media.

A JUICY GREEN TERRARIUM OF HAWORTHIA

There are said to be about 500 types of Haworthia, all of which have attractively fleshy, lustrous green leaves. Similar types planted together appear dull, so the trick is to combine several types with different forms, sizes, shades and textures, as shown here.

Layout

Plants to use

Haworthia reinwardtii—a
Haworthia turgida—b
Haworthia umbraticola—c
Haworthia cymbiformis (variegated)—d
Haworthia viscosa—e

You will need

Spherical glass container
White silicate soil
Seramis—f
Crushed coral (medium and small)—g
Natural stones (white, large)

Instructions

1 Place a small amount of white silicate soil into the container.

2 If more height is needed, add Seramis.

3 With the composition in mind, position plants to achieve a balanced look.

4 Hold plants firmly so they don't move, adding Seramis around them to secure.

5 Use tweezers to adjust positioning, adding in Seramis in the gaps in between plants.

6 Visualize a dividing line and add medium grains of coral to one side and small grains to the other. Complete by decorating with natural stones as desired.

TIPS

- Place near a window where air flows well and the light is about as bright as that filtered through lace curtains.
- Make sure Seramis and other matter doesn't cover the leaves as this will block the amount of light absorbed.

Plant Type

Haworthia

A WILD TERRARIUM PORTRAYING HAWORTHIA IN THEIR NATURAL DESERT HABITAT

This terrarium recreates the look of Haworthia growing gracefully on the slopes of the desert in southern Africa, depicting the abundant vitality of this arid region. Position taller plants at the back of the container and work smaller towards the front to create a feeling of balance in the slope.

Layout

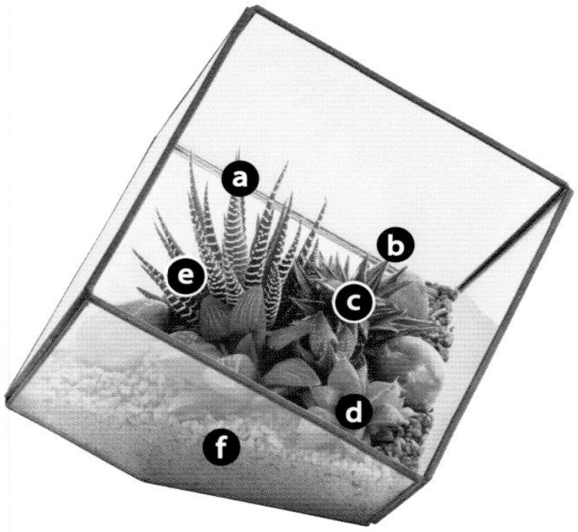

Instructions

1 Place a small amount of white silicate soil into the container.

2 Add in Seramis to create height at the back which decreases towards the front to form a moderate slope.

3 Secure plants, working from the back of the container.

4 Use tweezers to adjust plants' height and position.

5 Complete by decorating with natural stones as desired.

Plants to use

Haworthia attenuata—a
Haworthia starkiana (variegated)—b
Haworthia reinwardtii var. chalmnensis—c
Haworthia turgida—d
Haworthia retusa kotobuki—e

You will need

Tilted terrarium
White silicate sand
Seramis—f
Natural stones (large, brown)

TIPS

- It is easy for the soil to spill out from the front, so add slowly to avoid adding too much.
- When watering, use a spray bottle to prevent water spilling out of the container.
- Place in a spot near a window that gets good air flow and where the light is about as bright as that filtered through lace curtains.

250ml
600
250ml

SUCCULENTS IN A GROUPING OF BEAKERS

The go-to when it comes to terrarium containers, a beaker looks lonely on its own but is really appealing when grouped with several others of different sizes and shapes. Watering and other care can be adjusted to suit each plant in its individual beaker, so even plants requiring different growth environments can be placed together and thrive.

Layout

Plants to use

Haworthia umbraticola—a
Crassula tetragona—b
Pachyveria momobijin—c
Sedum rubrotinctum—d

You will need

Beakers
White silicate soil
Seramis—e
Pumice (medium grain)—f
Fuji sand—g

Instructions

1 Place a small amount of white silicate soil into each beaker.

2 Decide how high to position plants and pour Seramis into beakers.

3 Place plants in beakers and add more Seramis around plants to secure them. a

4 Finish by using tweezers or other tools to adjust the overall composition. b

※Use Fuji sand for Sedum rubrotinctum and pumice for Crassula tetragona.

TIPS

- Haworthia should be grown by a window where the light is about as bright as that filtered through a lace curtain. Make sure they receive plenty of sunlight but keep them out of direct sun during midsummer.
- These plants will not take root in beds composed only of pumice, volcanic ash and the like, so if cultivating them, use Seramis instead.

セダム
Sedum

Plant Type

Sedum

DELIGHTFUL DENSE-LEAF FORMATIONS IN A BOTTLE

The dense form created by its round, fleshy leaves makes the Sedum an attractive plant. This type grows vertically, so admire them in a bottle that has good height.

Layout

Instructions

1 Place a small amount of white silicate soil into the container.

2 Decide how high to position plants and pour Seramis into container.

3 Place plants in container and add Seramis around them to secure. ⓐ

4 Finish by using tweezers or other tools to adjust the overall composition.

Plants to use

Sedum treleasei—ⓐ

You will need

Wide-mouth glass bottle
White silicate soil
Seramis—ⓑ

TIP

■ As the mouth of the container is still relatively narrow, be careful when placing or removing plants to avoid damaging them.

Plant Type

Gasteria

FLESHY LEAVES AND FLOWERS FAN OUT FROM A GROUP OF GASTERIA

The Gasteria's flowers have the supple loveliness of Lily of the Valley, making a charming contrast to the plant's thick and fleshy leaves. These plants do well in a growing environment similar to that of Haworthia plants.

Layout

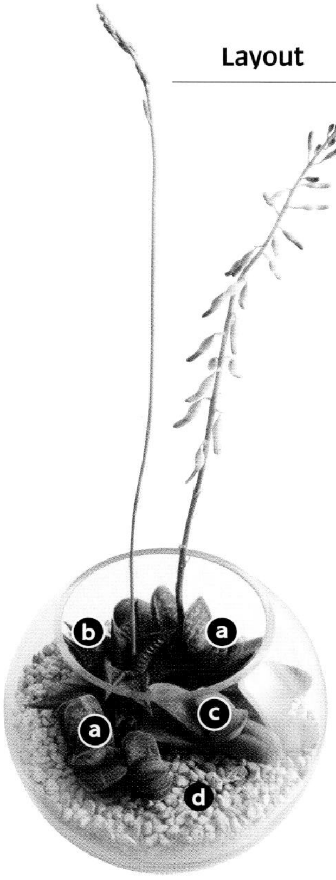

Instructions

1 Place a small amount of white silicate soil into the container, then add pumice.

2 Decide on the composition and position plants to achieve a balanced look.

3 Make seedlings stable so they don't move out of place, securing with Seramis.

4 Use tweezers to adjust positioning, adding Seramis in the gaps in-between plants. ⓐ

Plants to use

Gasteria gracilis var. minima (variegated)—ⓐ
Haworthia limifolia—ⓑ
Gasteria glomerata—ⓒ

You will need

Spherical glass container
White silicate soil (such as pumice)
Pumice—ⓓ
Seramis

TIPS

- These plants can be grown indoors with little light, but move them occasionally to a spot near a window so that they can receive light equivalent to that filtered through a lace curtain.
- Plants will not take root in a bed of pumice, so if cultivating them, use Seramis instead.

COMPLEMENTING A TERRARIUM OF CURLED ECHEVERIA WITH OTHER SMALLER VARIETIES

The charm of an Echeveria topsy turvy lies in its curled leaves. Choose one with large leaves to play the leading role, adding smaller-leaved types as supporting cast to set off the main plant. These types turn red around fall, creating a changing scenery for you to enjoy.

Layout

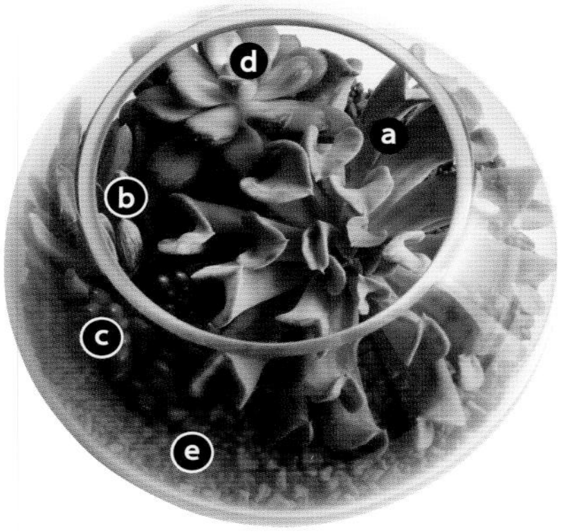

Plants to use

Echeveria topsy turvy—a
Senecio serpens—b
Sedum rubrotinctum—c
Graptoveria amethorum—d

You will need

Spherical glass container
White silicate soil
Seramis—e

Instructions

1 Place a small amount of white silicate soil into the container, then add Seramis.

2 Decide where to position Echeveria and secure it in place. a

3 Decide on positioning for other plants and secure them in place. b

4 Use tweezers to adjust overall balance, at the same time adding Seramis between plants to complete the terrarium.

TIPS

- Apart from during the direct sunlight of midsummer, make sure these plants get plenty of sun.
- Water has a tendency to collect in the leaves of the rosettes and cause sun damage. Use a spray bottle to water or direct water into the soil instead.

TINY CUTTINGS OF SUCCULENTS ARRANGED IN YOUR FAVORITE GLASS CONTAINERS

Another attractive aspect of succulents is how easily they can be multiplied by taking cuttings. A compact terrarium can be made by arranging a collection of cuttings taken from mature plants. Find a container that appeals to you and start planting!

Layouts

[A]

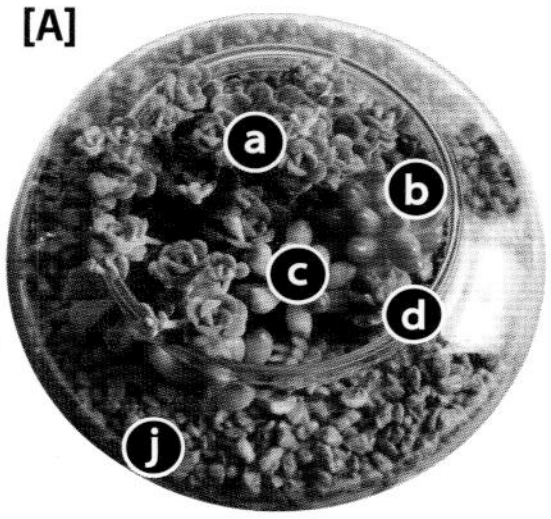

[B]

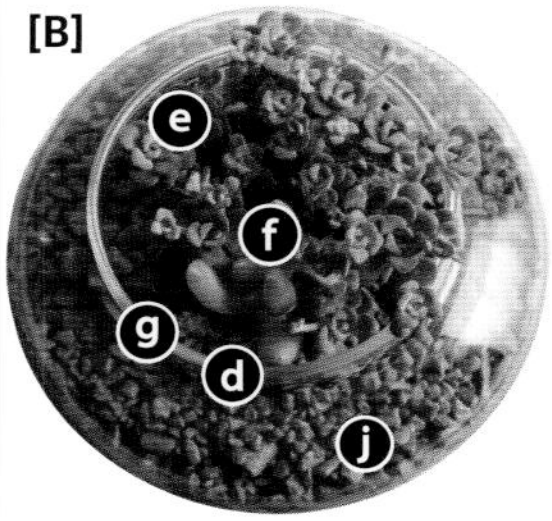

[C]

Plants to use

[A]
Sedum cape blanco—a
Sedum rubrotinctum—b
Sedum pachyphyllum —c
Sedum humifusum—d

[B]
Sedum cape blanco—e
Sedum golden glow—f
Graptopetalum copper rose—g
Sedum humifusum—d

[C]
Graptoveria titubans—h
Crassula conjuncta—i

You will need

Apothecary jars
White silicate soil
Seramis—j

Instructions

1 Place a small amount of white silicate soil into each container.

2 Decide how high to position plants and pour Seramis into each container.

3 Use tools such as tweezers to insert plants and secure them in place to complete the terrarium. a b

a

b

TIPS

- For containers that can be sealed, leave the lid off during the day to allow air in, but replace it at night so that water recirculates.
- Apart from the direct sun of midsummer, make sure the plants receive enough sun.

TERRARIUMS WITH LOVELY CHANGING LEAVES

Some types of succulents sport a lustrous green all year round, while others turn myriad shades around fall. Try planting groups of the same type together and enjoy experiencing their daily development.

Layouts

[A]

[B]

Plants to use

[A]
Haworthia koteki nishiki—a
Haworthia obtusa—b
Gasteria gracilis var. minima (variegated)—c

[B]
Sedum adolphii—d
Crassula ovata—e
Graptopetalum copper rose—f
Echeveria harmsii—g

You will need

Small glass jars
White silicate soil
Seramis—h
Pumice—i
Natural stones (small and medium, white)

Instructions

1 Place a small amount of white silicate soil into the container.

2 Add extra Seramis in areas where height is desired.

3 Decide on the composition and position plants to achieve a balanced look.

4 Hold plants so they can't slip out of place and add Seramis around them to secure them in position.

5 Use tweezers to adjust positioning and add pumice.

6 Add natural stones as decoration to complete. a

a

TIPS

- For containers that can be sealed, leave the lid off during the day to allow air in, but replace it at night so that water recirculates.
- Place terrarium [A] near a window to receive light about as bright as that filtered through a lace curtain. For terrarium [B], apart from the direct sunlight of midsummer, make sure it receives plenty of sun.

Plant Type

Echeveria

FRESH FRAGRANCE OF AROMATICUS IN YOUR OWN LITTLE BOX GARDEN

This little garden incorporates Aromaticus, which is named for its delightful fragrance. Placing natural stones on a bed of Seramis and arranging large stones to resemble rocks expands the scenic possibilities. Try selecting plants with similar growth habitats to create your very own combinations!

Layout

Plants to use

Plectranthus amboinicus—a
Echeveria kirchneriana—b
Echeveria opal—c
Crassula sarmentosa—d

You will need

House-shaped terrarium
White silicate sand
Pumice —e
Seramis—f
Natural stones (medium, gray)
Natural stones (large, black)

Instructions

1 Place a small amount of white silicate soil into the container, then add pumice.

2 Decide how high to position plants and pour Seramis into container.

3 Working from the back of the container, secure plants in order of height with the tallest first.

4 Use tweezers to adjust plants' height and position.

5 Lay down medium sized natural stones and position larger stones as desired to complete.

TIPS

- Leave the doors open during the day to allow air in, but close them at night so that water recirculates.
- Apart from the direct sun of midsummer, make sure the plants receive enough sun.

Layouts

[A]

[B]

[C]

Plants to use

[A] Crassula marnieriana—a
[B] Sedum treleasei—b
[C] Sedum rubrotinctum—c

You will need

Cylindrical glass containers
White silicate soil
Natural stones (small, purple)

Plant Type

Sedum

EXOTIC MINI TERRARIUMS USING CUTTINGS FROM OTHER MINI PLANTS

It's fun preparing the soil beds for cuttings taken from mini plants. Using purple or dark reddish natural stones instantly results in an exotic look. Try different arrangements and settings to match your surroundings.

Instructions

1 Place a small amount of white silicate soil into each container.

2 Decide how high to position plants and add natural stones.

3 Use tweezers to insert plants into soil bed.

4 Place natural stones around plants to complete. (a)

TIPS

- Do not water until cuttings have started to take root.
- If cultivating plants, use white silicate soil, Seramis and similar to create soil bed.

Plant Type
Haworthia

THE ROUND SHAPE AND JEWEL-LIKE SPARKLE OF HAWORTHIA OBTUSA IN A GLOBE TERRARIUM

Charmingly plump, Haworthia obtusa has a calming effect on the viewer. Some Haworthias have translucent "windows" at the tips of their leaves which absorb sunlight, and the obtusa's leaf windows are particularly lovely. Try holding one up to the light—both the leaves and the overall plant look magical.

Layout

Instructions

1 Place a small amount of white silicate soil into the container.

2 If height is desired, add a large amount of Seramis.

3 Place plant in center of container and add Seramis around it to secure.

4 Position bark as desired to complete. ⓐ

Plants to use

Haworthia obtusa with large rounded leaves—ⓐ

You will need

Spherical glass container
White silicate soil
Seramis—ⓑ
Bark

TIP

- Place in a spot near a window that gets good air flow and where the light is about as bright as that filtered through lace curtains.

STRIKING RED BLOSSOMS IN A TERRARIUM OF EUPHORBIA

At a glance, this plant doesn't appear to be a succulent, but if you look at the stem you'll see it's fleshy and covered in thorns. The pretty bright red flowers (flower bracts) have made this a popular plant from way back. Multiple varieties mean the flowers come in different colors, so find one to suit your taste.

Layouts

[A]

[B]

Plants to use

[A]
Euphorbia milii (red)—a

[B]
Haworthia vittata—b

You will need

Cylindrical glass containers
White silicate soil
Seramis—c

Instructions

1 Place a small amount of white silicate soil into the container.

2 Decide how high to position plant and pour Seramis into container.

3 Secure plants in the center of each container and use tweezers to adjust position and complete the terrariums. a b

TIPS

- The Euphorbia's white sap can cause inflammation if touched, so handle with care.
- Leave open during the day to allow air in, but if possible cover opening at night so that water recirculates.
- Place near a window that gets light about as bright as that filtered through lace curtains. Euphorbia should occasionally be placed in sunlight—as long as it is gentle sunlight.

practical tip
3

FINDING THE PERFECT CONTAINER

One of the things that makes terrariums so appealing is the fun of choosing your containers. Try a little treasure hunting and artful repurposing to create terrariums reflecting your own personal taste.

TERRARIUMS DON'T HAVE TO COST MUCH. YOU CAN FIND CONTAINERS AND OTHER MATERIALS EVEN AT DOLLAR STORES

In recent years, some dollar stores have added gardening sections. Some of these include plants as well as containers, so it's possible to create terrariums just with goods that can be found in these stores. Their low prices make it affordable to experiment with different materials, such as ornamental sand and bark to decorate terrarium surfaces.

INTERIOR DESIGN STORES

Interior design stores carry purpose-made terrarums of all kinds, but when shopping in these stores, browse with an open mind as to what other types of container may used for a terrarium. Be sure to visit the kitchen, tableware, candle and bath sections. You may discover lots of new possibilities.

THRIFT STORES AND CRAFT STORES

Nothing is more charming than a vintage glass container, or even one that just looks vintage. Old jars, glassware and vases are just the beginning. Vintage light globes, hurricane lamps, lanterns, decanters and so many other items can be used to make truly unique terrariums.

Like interior design stores, craft stores sell glass globes, bowls, even beakers and flasks made specifically for terrarium planting and other home decor projects.

GARDENING STORES

Gardening stores are goof-proof when it comes to finding the best containers for cultivation. Standard containers such as round or cylindrical types make watering and soil maintenance easy. If grouping several plants together, using a container with a wide mouth makes it easy to create the plants' layout, so a simple container from a gardening store is recommended. And the staff are usually happy to share their expertise.

repurpose!

simple is best!

Chapter 4

MIXED TERRARIUMS

Moss, air plants and succulents are planted together in these terrariums. Combining types sets off the beauty of each individual plant while harmonizing the balance of the plants together. The results are strikingly beautiful.

Plant Types

Echeveria + Moss + Fern

USE DARK TONES TO CREATE A SENSE OF CALM: A TERRARIUM WITH SUCCULENTS, MOSS & FERNS

Dark tones are the ties that bind in a terrarium in which a large Echeveria plays the leading role. The trick to creating it is to position the plants from the center outward. Allowing a charming heart-shaped leaf to protrude from the container lends dimension.

Layout

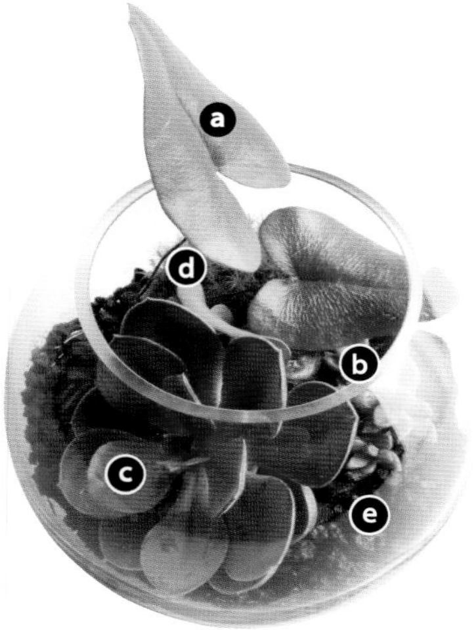

Plants to use

Heart fern—a
Graptosedum bronze—b
Echeveria opal—c
Bartramia pomiformis—d

You will need

Spherical glass container
White silicate soil
Fuji sand—e

Instructions

1 Place a small amount of white silicate soil into the container, then use gravel such as Fuji sand.

2 With an image of the completed terrarium in mind, position all plants except moss to achieve a balanced look.

3 Secure the plants with potting mix still attached to the roots, adding Fuji sand in around them.

4 Use tweezers to adjust positioning and add Fuji sand between plants. a

5 Add moss to complete. b

TIPS

- Succulents enjoy direct sunlight except in midsummer, so as much as possible, position the terrarium so that only the succulents receive sunlight.
- Use a spray bottle to water ferns and mosses so they do not dry out.

A WETLAND TERRARIUM OF SHADOW-LOVING PLANTS WITH PAPHIOPEDILUM IN THE LEADING ROLE

This mixed terrarium brings together plants from three different habitats. The trick to maintaining this type of terrarium is to use the bottom layer of gravel to judge the timing for watering.

Layout

Plants to use

Pteris—a
Haworthia umbraticola—b
Haworthia viscosa—c
Paphiopedilum—d
Hypnaceae—e

You will need

Jar-type glass container
White silicate soil
Pumice (medium grain)—f
Potting mix
Granular medium based on charcoal and porous ceramic material—g

Instructions

1 Place a small amount of white silicate soil into the container, then cover with a layer of pumice to form a base.

2 Decide how high to position plants and pour potting mix into container.

3 Decide where the front of the terrarium will be. With the exception of moss, secure all plants with granular medium, working from the tallest plants first.

4 Use tweezers to adjust the overall composition.

5 Finish by laying down moss. a

a

TIPS

- Keep out of direct sun. If growing outdoors, place in a bright but shaded place. If growing indoors, place near a window in a spot that is well ventilated and receives light as bright as that filtered through a lace curtain.
- With the exception of succulents, use a spray bottle to make sure plants get plenty of water and do not dry out.

CUTE ROSETTES THAT TURN PINK: A TERRARIUM WITH MOSS, AIR PLANTS & SUCCULENTS

Anchored by rosette-shaped succulents, this group planting brings together relatively low-growing specimens that can be admired from any angle. In the fall, the succulents' leaves change colors, creating the illusion of flowers blooming.

Layout

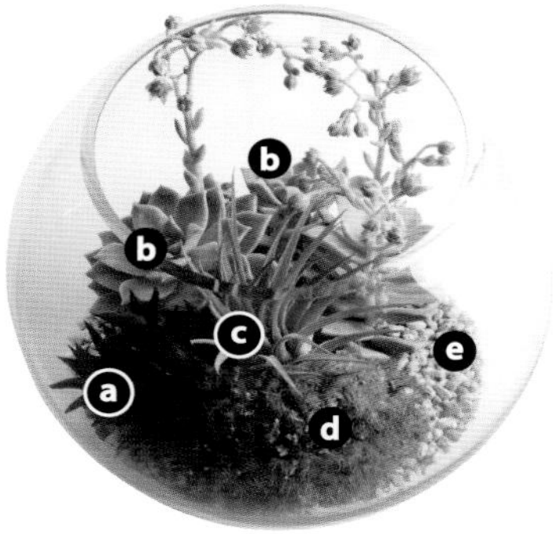

Plants to use

Haworthia tortuosa—a
Echeveria white rose—b
Tillandsia ionantha—c
Bartramia pomiformis—d

You will need

Spherical glass container
White silicate soil
Potting mix
Pumice (medium grain)—e

Instructions

1 Place a small amount of white silicate soil into the container, then cover with a layer of pumice to form a base.

2 With the finished result in mind, use pumice to secure succulents which still have potting mix attached.

3 Lay down moss.

4 Add air plants. a

5 Finish by using tweezers or other tools to adjust the overall composition. b

TIP

- The plants' watering requirements differ, so use the spray bottle to give plenty of water only to the plants that need it. Remove the ionantha from the terrarium to water it.

MULTI-HUED GREENS GLOW IN A TRIPLE-MIX TERRARIUM

Plants with leaves that differ in form, feel and texture are grouped together here to create a miniature botanical garden. Building the Selaginella and Bartramia pomiformis up high and placing smaller plants at the front creates an attractive ensemble.

Layout

Plants to use

Selaginella—a
Bartramia pomiformis—b
Tillandsia fuchsii var gracilis—c
Cotyledon pendens—d
Haworthia starkiana (variegated)—e

You will need

Tilted terrarium
White silicate soil
Potting mix
Pumice (medium grain)—f

Instructions

1 Place a small amount of white silicate soil into the container.

2 Place pumice in container so it forms a high mound at the back that slopes gently down to the front.

3 With the completed result in mind, place Selaginella with potting mix still attached at the back of the container and secure with pumice.

4 Next, secure succulents, working from the back to the front, and attach moss. a

5 Add air plants. b

6 Finish by using tweezers to adjust the overall composition.

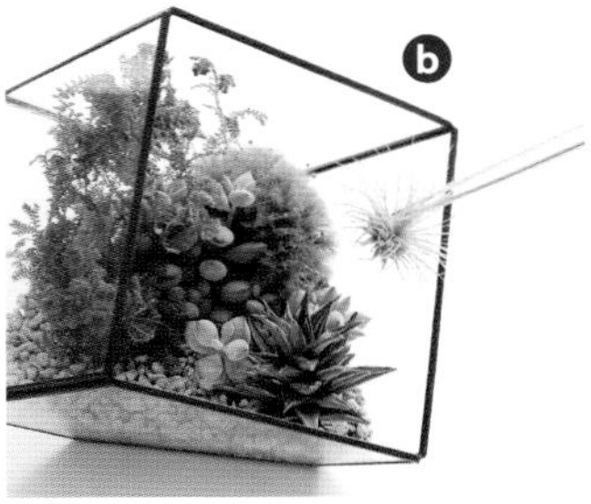

TIPS

- Apart from during midsummer, Cotyledons enjoy direct sunlight. Position the terrarium so that the Cotyledon is in the brightest spot in the room.
- The plants' watering requirements differ, so use the spray bottle to give plenty of water only to the plants that need it. Remove the fuchsii var gracilis from the terrarium to water it.

CATALOG OF SUCCULENTS

Here, we introduce some of the succulents used in this book. Their different growth periods (spring/fall, summer and winter) should be taken into account when creating a terrarium.

ECHEVERIA
CRASSULACEAE FAMILY

This family of plants is characterized by its flamboyance. It comes in various colors and shapes, so abundant variation can be achieved even in a terrarium composed exclusively of echeveria.

Echeveria topsy turvy

[Spring/fall grower] This type gets its name from its leaves, which appear to be attached the wrong way around. In the fall, the entire plant turns a pale pink. ▶Used on p64

Echeveria kirchneriana

[Spring/fall grower] The leaf tips of this succulent are a subtle shade of pink. It has orange flowers. ▶Used on p70

Echeveria harmsii

[Summer grower] Also known as the plush plant, it is characterized by its leaves, which are covered in a light fuzz. In the fall, the leaves turn red at the tips and create an attractive contrast with the green. ▶Used on p68

Echeveria opal

[Summer grower] This fleshy succulent has beautiful purple leaves. As its leaves remain this color year-round, it works well as an accent in a terrarium. ▶Used on p70, p80

HAWORTHIA
LILIACEAE FAMILY

In the translucent varieties, the leaf tips act as lenses, turning the entire plant a clear green. Hardy against cold and heat, it's a genus that is easy to grow.

Haworthia cymbiformis (variegated)

[Spring/fall grower] The yellow running through the green leaves and the translucent "windows" at the leaf tips are typical of a Haworthia. In comparison with other succulents, these plants favor shaded areas. ▶Used on p54

Haworthia viscosa

[Spring/fall grower] This type is defined by its trio of leaves that grow in layers. Its deep, serene green color provides an accent when incorporated into a terrarium of vivid verdant tones. ▶Used on p54, p82

Haworthia turgida

[Spring/fall grower] This Haworthia has tough yellow-green leaves. It maintains its color year-round, but be aware of its vulnerability to strong light. ▶Used on p54, p56

Haworthia attenuate

[Spring/fall grower] White horizontal stripes are the defining characteristic of this thick-leaved type. Even within the same type, some of the white stripes are broad and others are finer, so choose a specimen that complements the other plants you are using. ▶Used on p56

Haworthia retusa kotobuki

[Spring/fall grower] Vertical white markings define this type. Although somber in coloring and small in stature, this is a plant with plenty of presence. ▶Used on p56

Haworthia vittata

[Spring/fall grower] The juicy green shade of this plant is eye-catching. It dislikes strong light, so it is recommended to grow it with Haworthias, Gasterias and other plants that need to be kept out of direct sunlight. ▶Used on p76

SEDUM
CRASSULACEAE FAMILY

Even among succulents, the Sedum genus stands out for its many varieties and chubby leaves. All its varieties are hardy, making it an easy plant for beginners to grow.

Sedum rubrotinctum

[Spring/fall grower] Both the chubby leaves and the stem of this plant are hardy, and as it is suited to being grown from cuttings, even beginners will find it easy to grow. In this variety, the combination of hues is especially attractive when the leaves change color. ▶Used on p58, p64, p66, p72

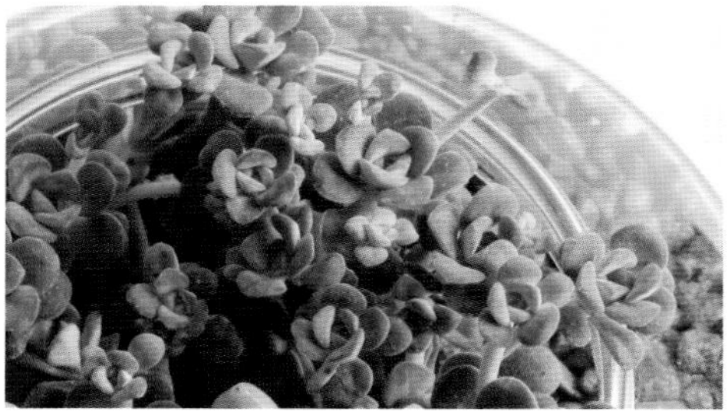

Sedum cape blanco

[Spring/fall grower] This Sedum grows in a dome shape. Its entire surface is powdery white, with yellow flowers blooming in spring. It likes the cold but is vulnerable in summer, so care is needed. ▶Used on p66

Sedum pachyphyllum

[Spring/fall grower] This type gets its Japanese name, "Maiden's mind" from the blush of pink that appears at the tip of the leaves when they change color. It works as an accent in a terrarium. ▶Used on p66

Sedum golden glow

[Spring/fall grower] This type does not change color, maintaining a yellow hue all year round. For this reason, it can be planted with other Sedum to create a delightful color scheme. ▶Used on p66

Sedum adolphii

[spring/fall grower] A glossy yellow color characterizes this type. ▶Used on p68

Sedum treleasei

[Spring/fall grower] Plump, vibrant blue-green leaves define this type. ▶Used on p72

GASTERIA
LILIACEAE FAMILY

While most succulents are hardy, this is a particularly hardy genus. Patterns form on the center of the fleshy leaves and it also flowers. The flowers' resemblance to a stomach (Latin: gaster) is what gives the plant its name.

Gasteria gracilis var. minima (variegated)

[Summer grower] The patchy patterns on the leaves define this variety. ▶Used on p62

Gasteria glomerata

[Summer grower] This Gasteria has plump, rounded orange flowers and whitish-tinged leaves. ▶Used on p62

CRASSULA
CRASSULACEAE FAMILY

These plants are characterized by their charming flower petals. The varieties whose leaves are fleshy and covered in fuzz are vulnerable to heat, so it's important to keep them well ventilated and water sparingly.

Crassula tetragona

[Summer grower] This type is defined by the way it grows, stretching upwards. The stem becomes woodier as it grows. ▶Used on p58

Crassula sarmentosa

[Summer grower] The leaves of this type turn red around the edges in the fall. The stem turns red and grows in a vertical direction. ▶Used on p70

Crassula ovata

[Spring/fall grower] The round, thick shape of the leaves gives rise to this plant's alternative name, money tree. It is defined by the red tinge at the tips of the leaves. ▶Used on p68

Crassula marnieriana

[Summer grower] This succulent is characterized by the winding fashion in which it grows. Grow it in combination with plants twisting in different directions for an attractive result. ▶Used on p72

CATALOG OF AIR PLANTS

There are said to be more than 600 original species of air plant, and more than 2000 types when cultivated varieties are included. Only a few are presented here to illustrate the characteristics of air plants in this book.

Tillandsia Ionantha

In comparison with other varieties, these are hardy and easy for beginners to grow. The leaves turn steadily red as the plant enters its bloom cycle and starts to flower. It is one of the most popular varieties of air plants. ▶Used on p32, p34, p46, p84

Tillandsia capitata red

This silver-leaved variety is found widely from Central America through to South America. Of all the capitata varieties, this is the reddest. Keep it out of direct sunlight to maintain the color.
▶Used on p36

Tillandsia usneoides (Spanish moss)

Although it grows by absorbing moisture from the air through the surface of its leaves, the body of the plant is too delicate to store it, so make sure to water regularly. ▶Used on p36, p46, p50

Tillandsia aeranthos

This variety is resistant not only to heat and cold but also to dehydration. At the start of spring, it blooms with bluish purple flowers, making it visually attractive and ideal for beginners.
▶Used on p32, p42, p44

Tillandsia caput-medusae

This plant gets its name from the Medusa of Greek myth. It is characterized by its base section, which resembles an urn. ▶Used on p42

Tillandsia harrisii

This type flowers once it reaches about 8 inch (20cm) or so. It is hardy and easy to grow. Trichomes on its surface make it appear white. ▶Used on p46

Tillandsia andreana

The super-fine leaves spread out in a radial fashion in this rare variety, also known as the jewel of the Tillandsia. It is vulnerable in cold climates, so is best grown in a greenhouse. ▶Used on p44

Tillandsia fuchsii var gracilis

The delicate strand-like flowers are the most defining characteristic of this plant. It begins to wither in low humidity so if growing it indoors, it is crucial to make sure it doesn't dry out.
▶Used on p40, p50, p86

Tillandsia stricta

Flowering is nearly an annual event for this type, which, for an air plant, is relatively fond of water. Cultivating in a pot is recommended. ▶Used on p48

Tillandsia cyanea

Hailing from Central South America, this flowering plant is also called the Pink Quill for its "feather" of bright pink bracts from which blue or purple flowers sometimes bloom. ▶Used on p44

MOSS AND OTHER WETLAND PLANTS

This section features wetland-loving plants, such as ferns and moss. Moss in particular looks attractive even when grown on its own and is an ideal terrarium plant.

Selaginella

Also known as cushion moss, this plant does not cope well with dehydration, so make sure it is well watered regardless of the season. ▶Used on p16, p18, p22, p24, p86

Ficus pumila

A member of the Moraceae family, this plant has white or yellow mottling on its leaves. It is resilient against cold and likes water, making it suitable for hydroculture. ▶Used on p18

Butterwort

This carnivorous plant's leaves are covered in a viscous liquid that contains digestive enzymes. Its purple flowers create a visual accent when it is planted together with moss.
▶Used on p26

Pteris

There are over 275 species of this fern. In a terrarium, its coloring and form create the impression of coolness. It does not like the cold, so grow it in a bright, shaded area.
▶Used on p26, p82

Bartramia pomiformis

This yellow-green moss grows in clumps in wetland areas. It has spherical spore capsules. ▶Used on p20, 22, 80, 84, 86

Bryum argenteum

This moss is yellow-green to a silvery green in color, with comparatively thick foliage. As long as there is high humidity, it can be grown even in very sunny areas. It can be gathered from footpaths, grassy areas and so on. ▶Used on p18

Rainbow fan (Selaginella uncinata)

This member of the Selaginella family has vivid green leaves that change color depending on how the light hits them, lending it its common name. It copes well with cold. ▶Used on p18

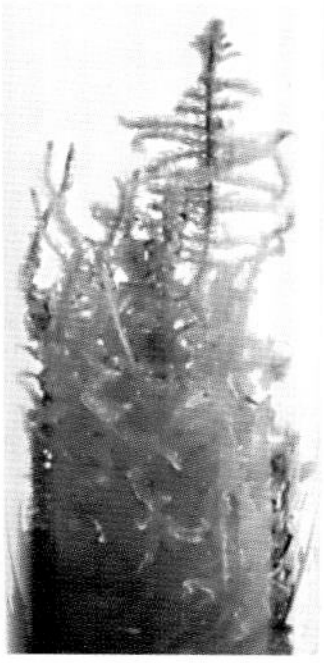

Hypnaceae

This miniature moss is often used as a ground covering for bonsai. It is found all over the world and can be found at the side of paths, on stone walls and many other places. ▶Used on p22, p26, p82

Paphiopedilum

A pouch forms part of the flower in this plant, a genus of the orchid family. It copes well with low temperatures and likes wetland areas. It grows even in weak sunlight. ▶Used on p82

Published by Tuttle Publishing, an imprint of Periplus Editions (HK) Ltd.

www.tuttlepublishing.com

ISBN 978 4 8053 1477 7

TERRARIUM KOKE, AIRPLANTS, TANIKUSHOKUBUTSU DE TSUKURU

Translated from Japanese by Leeyong Soo

Supervising editor: Eriko Terui, FOURWORDS, ACTUS Shinjuku branch. Managing director, indoor plant specialty store FOURWORDS. Responsible for OASIS PLANTS located within the Shinjuku branch of interior store ACTUS. Advises on indoor plants, focusing on succulents and air plants.

Staff
Photography: Miyuki Teraoka
Styling: Aoi Maruyama
Design: Naoko Yamada (Studio Dank)
Text cooperation: Rie Kishima
Editing & layout: Ryo Fujii, Yumi Ebinuma (Studio Dank)
Planning & layout: Takashi Makino
Production management: Nakagawa Watanabe
Special thanks: Tsukamoto

Distributed by

North America, Latin America & Europe
Tuttle Publishing
364 Innovation Drive, North Clarendon,
VT 05759-9436 U.S.A.
Tel: 1 (802) 773-8930; Fax: 1 (802) 773-6993
info@tuttlepublishing.com; www.tuttlepublishing.com

Japan
Tuttle Publishing
Yaekari Building, 3rd Floor, 5-4-12 Osaki,
Shinagawa-ku, Tokyo 141 0032
Tel: (81) 3 5430171; Fax: (81) 3 5437-0755
sales@tuttle.co.jp; www.tuttle.co.jp

Asia Pacific
Berkeley Books Pte. Ltd.
61 Tai Seng Avenue #02-12, Singapore 534167
Tel: (65) 6280-1330; Fax: (65) 6280-6290
inquiries@periplus.com.sg; www.periplus.com

Printed in China 1712RR
21 20 19 18 10 9 8 7 6 5 4 3 2 1

ABOUT TUTTLE "BOOKS TO SPAN THE EAST AND WEST"

Our core mission at Tuttle Publishing is to create books which bring people together one page at a time. Tuttle was founded in 1832 in the small New England town of Rutland, Vermont (USA). Our fundamental values remain as strong today as they were then—to publish best-in-class books informing the English-speaking world about the countries and peoples of Asia. The world has become a smaller place today and Asia's economic, cultural and political influence has expanded, yet the need for meaningful dialogue and information about this diverse region has never been greater. Since 1948, Tuttle has been a leader in publishing books on the cultures, arts, cuisines, languages and literatures of Asia. Our authors and photographers have won numerous awards and Tuttle has published thousands of books on subjects ranging from martial arts to paper crafts. We welcome you to explore the wealth of information available on Asia at **www.tuttlepublishing.com.**